MY BEST BOOK

DINOSAURS

Christopher Maynard

KINGFISHER
LONDON & NEW YORK

KINGFISHER
LONDON & NEW YORK

Copyright © Macmillan Publishers International 2005, 2020
First published in 1995 in the United States by Kingfisher
This edition is published in 2020 by Kingfisher
120 Broadway, New York, NY 10271
Kingfisher is an imprint of Macmillan Children's Books, London
All rights reserved.

Distributed in the U.S. and Canada by Macmillan,
120 Broadway, New York, NY 10271

Library of Congress Cataloguing-in-Publication data
has been applied for.

ISBN 978-0-7534-7540-9

Design by Jake da'Costa & Intrepid Books Ltd
Illustrations: Illustrations: James Field, Chris Forsey,
Christian Hook, Steve Kirk

Kingfisher books are available for special promotions and
premiums. For details contact: Special Markets Department,
Macmillan, 120 Broadway, New York, NY 10271.

For more information please visit
www.kingfisherbooks.com

Printed in China

10 9 8 7 6 5 4 3 2 1
1TR/1119/UNTD/WKT/128MA

Picture credits
The Publisher would like to thank the following for permission
to reproduce their material.
Top = t; Bottom = b; Center = c; Left = l; Right = r
p1 Shutterstock/kikujungboy; 2–3, 32 Shutterstock/
Warpaint; 4–5 bg (background) Shuttersstock/BGSmith; 4bl
Shutterstock/Catmando; 5t Shutterstock/Shvoeva Elena; 5b
Shutterstock/Giedriius, 5b Shutterstock/Giedriius; 6–7 bg
Flickr/Ian Westcott; 8, 16, 22–23 iStock/Warpaintcobra; 8–9
bg iStock/sbayram; 10–11 bg iStock/Dimitris66; 12–13 bg
Shutterstock/Kostyantyn Ivanyshen; 14–15 bg Shutterstock/
Charcompix; 16–17 bg iStock/4kodiak; 17 iStock/
digitalgenetics; 18 Shutterstock/Herschel Hoffmeyer; 18–19
iStock/Daniel Eskridge; 20–21 bg iStock/CoreyFord; 22–23
bg Shutterstock/Cameron Best; 24bl, 24 br iStock/Elenarts;
24–25 bg Shutterstock/Andrii Lutsyk; 26–27 Shutterstock/
Herschel Hoffmeyer; 28–29 bg Shutterstock/chalermkeat
chall; 30–31bg iStock/Wicki58.

CONTENTS

DINOSAUR BABIES

Imagine the world 75 million years ago.
This Maiasaura mother dinosaur has guarded
her eggs for many weeks. Now, one by one,
her babies crack through their shell and wriggle
out into their nest. Some stop to nibble at the
blanket of rotting plants that has kept them warm.
Others take their first look at their incredible world.

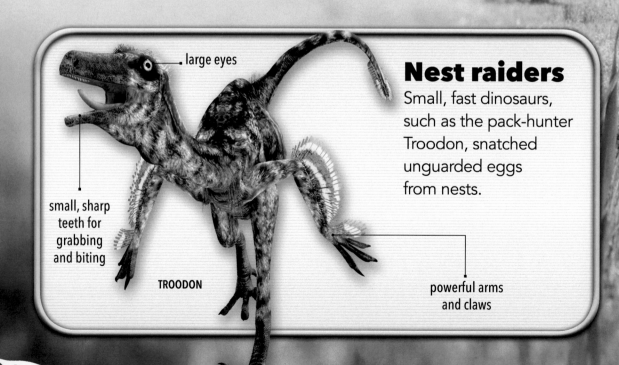

large eyes

small, sharp
teeth for
grabbing
and biting

TROODON

Nest raiders

Small, fast dinosaurs,
such as the pack-hunter
Troodon, snatched
unguarded eggs
from nests.

powerful arms
and claws

FROM EGG TO ADULT

Most dinosaurs laid their eggs in a nest. A few, like Maiasaura, built their nests together, in a group or colony. Every year, they returned to the same place to lay their eggs.

Dinosaur eggs

Dinosaurs were reptiles and they laid all kinds of egg, just like today's reptiles do. The biggest were the size of a football.

Hypselosaurus
11 ½ in (30cm)

Protoceratops
8 in (20cm)

Maiasaura
4 ½ in (12cm)

Growing up

1. First, a female Maiasaura dug a large, round hole, about the size of a backyard wading pool but much deeper.

2. Then she laid up to 20 eggs, each with a soft, leathery shell. The eggs rolled to the bottom of the nest before Maiasaura covered them with a blanket of plants.

3. Maiasaura guarded her nest while the blanket of plants rotted, keeping the eggs warm.

4. She stayed alert all the time to scare away nest raiders.

5. Weeks later, the eggs cracked and the first babies hatched out. Within minutes, they could walk around and forage for food.

6. A young Maiasaura more than doubled in size by its first birthday. It had to be strong enough to keep up with its herd and survive.

LIVING IN HERDS

Most herd dinosaurs were peaceful plant-eaters, such as the enormous Apatosaurus. Safety in numbers was often the best defense against meat-eating dinosaurs. A large herd had hundreds of pairs of eyes. Some members of the herd were always on the lookout, ready to bellow a warning if they spotted a hunter.

On the move

An Apatosaurus herd would travel up to 25 miles (40km) per day to search for food.

APATOSAURUS

Defense strategies

When a herd was on the move, like these Iguanodon, babies walked in the middle, guarded by their parents on the outside.

If attacked, a Triceratops herd backed into a circle with the babies in the center and big males pointing their horns outward.

When a Lambeosaurus herd settled down to sleep, some dinosaurs stayed awake and moved around, like soldiers on guard duty.

In some herds, males fought for a female or to decide the herd leader. Pachycephalosaurus had a thick, dome-shaped skull to protect its brain during fights. The males crashed into each other until the weaker one ran away.

DUCK-BILLED DINOS

Duckbills had long, flat snouts, a little like a duck's bill. The family name for them is Hadrosaurs. Most duckbills had a bump, horn, or crest on their head, which they used to honk at the rest of the herd, signaling that all was well or warning that danger was ahead.

MALE PARASAUROLOPHUS

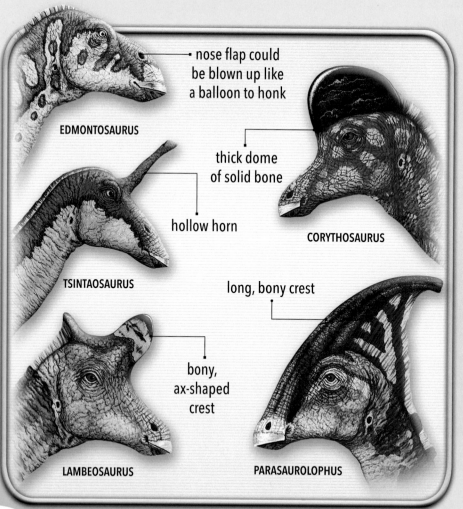

nose flap could be blown up like a balloon to honk

EDMONTOSAURUS

thick dome of solid bone

hollow horn

CORYTHOSAURUS

TSINTAOSAURUS

long, bony crest

bony, ax-shaped crest

LAMBEOSAURUS

PARASAUROLOPHUS

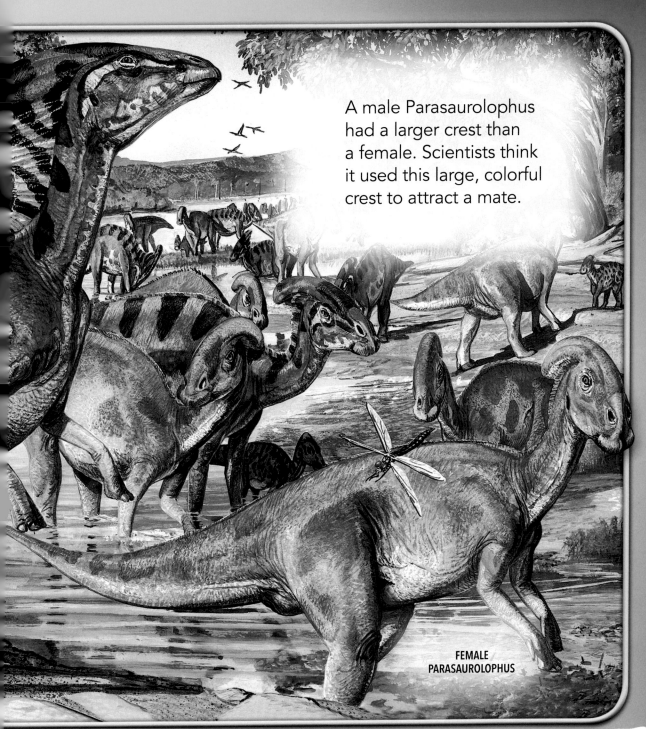

A male Parasaurolophus had a larger crest than a female. Scientists think it used this large, colorful crest to attract a mate.

FEMALE PARASAUROLOPHUS

LONG-NECKED DINOSAURS

A giant head swings up to the treetops, stripping away mouthfuls of leaves and twigs with its stumpy, peg-shaped teeth. It swallows everything, without chewing, down a neck as long as a telephone pole. This is Alamosaurus—a long-necked plant-eater belonging to a group of dinosaurs called Sauropods. Long-necks were some of the biggest animals ever to live on Earth.

BRACHIOSAURUS
85 ½ ft (26m) long

DIPLODOCUS
99 ft (30.2m) long

BAROSAURUS
95 ft (29m) long

TITANOSAURUS
45 ½ ft (13.9m) long

APATOSAURUS
80 ft (24.4m) long

Gentle giants

To see how long a Sauropod was, put this book on the floor and take 130 short steps (each as long as your foot) away from it. Now look back.

PEACEFUL PLANT-EATERS

Dinosaurs lived on Earth for nearly 160 million years. During that time, the climate changed. In the Triassic period, Earth was hot, dry, and covered in desert. Then came the Jurassic period, when the climate turned rainy, forming tropical swamps. Finally, Earth cooled over the Cretaceous period and forests of conifers grew. As Earth's climate changed, different plants developed and plant-eating dinosaurs changed to suit their new food.

Stomach stones

A Sauropod, such as Shunosaurus, would gulp down stones as it ate. The stones stayed in its gut, helping the stomach muscles grind leaves and twigs into a soft, sticky stew of plants, which could be easily digested.

Diets through time

SHUNOSAURUS

JURASSIC

165 million years ago, long-necked Shunosaurus used its peg-shaped teeth to chop tough branches, shoots, and needles.

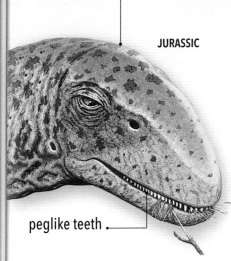

peglike teeth

CRETACEOUS

SAUROLOPHUS

hard beak

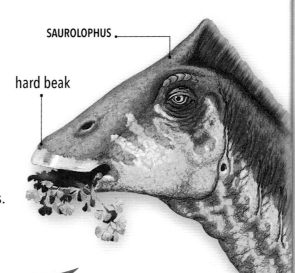

70 million years ago, duckbill Saurolophus used its beak to snip rubbery leaves from flowering shrubs.

LATE CRETACEOUS

TRICERATOPS

Around 68 million years ago, the horned dinosaur Triceratops used its pointed beak to pluck tough ferns and palms from the ground.

pointed beak

TERRIFYING TYRANNOSAURUS

Lurking in the shadows of a redwood forest, a giant Tyrannosaurus sniffs the breeze and grunts. It can smell food nearby. Then it spies a mother Edmontosaurus and two youngsters in a glade. The big hunter stalks them quietly. Then, when it is just 380 feet (116m) away, it erupts roaring from the trees. In just a few seconds, it is on them. Its huge, heavy jaws tear into one of the young dinosaurs with a wild, killing bite.

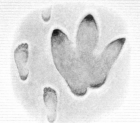

Quick foot

Tyrannosaurus had three toes, with a giant talon on each foot. Its footprint was two feet (0.6m) long—twice as long as a human's. It could run as fast as a horse, at almost 24mph (39kph).

MIGHTY MEAT-EATERS

TYRANNOSAURUS
REX

A full-grown Tyrannosaurus rex had about 50 razor-sharp teeth. Each tooth was as long as a banana, with a sharp point to stab its victim and rough edges to rip through skin and flesh.

DILOPHOSAURUS   ALLOSAURUS   ALBERTOSAURUS

Ferocious hunters

These fierce hunters were all related to Tyrannosaurus, with sharp teeth and claws. None, though, were quite as big. A Tyrannosaurus was tall enough to look through a second-floor window.

Going hunting

1. Allosaurus uses its small arms to balance as it rears up on its hind legs to rise from the ground.

2. Its last meal was four days ago. It tears into an old carcass, but there is little meat left to ease its hunger.

3. Its sharp eyes spot a herd of plant-eaters. Slowly it creeps up on them, waiting for the right moment.

4. A young dinosaur lags behind the herd. Allosaurus attacks, grabbing its victim by the neck and tearing out a huge slab of flesh in one lethal bite.

5. Allosaurus rips out chunk after chunk of flesh and bone and swallows them whole. It gorges till its belly is bloated. Then it staggers away to lie down and doze for hours.

PACK ATTACK!

Plant-eating Tenontosaurus weighed up to two tons but it was no match for a pack of attacking Deinonychus. The wolf-sized hunters would charge at Tenontosaurus from all sides, trying to slash open its hide with their giant claws. Their feathered arms flapped to keep them steady as they clung on to the struggling Tenontosaurus, biting chunks from its flesh.

DEINONYCHUS

Pack's prey
Tenontosaurus' main defenses would be to whip the attacking Deinonychus with its long, strong tail or crush them with its weight.

Terrible claw

Deinonychus had a long talon on each back foot, similar to an eagle's claw. Scientists think it may have attacked from above, using its talon to grab its prey, just like an eagle.

Deinonychus foot

Sickle-shaped talon

TENONTOSAURUS

ARMORED DINOSAURS

Plant-eaters had many ways of protecting themselves.
Some lived in herds and found safety in numbers. A few
were just too big to be attacked. Others had body armor
to defend themselves, and horns or spiked tails to fight with.

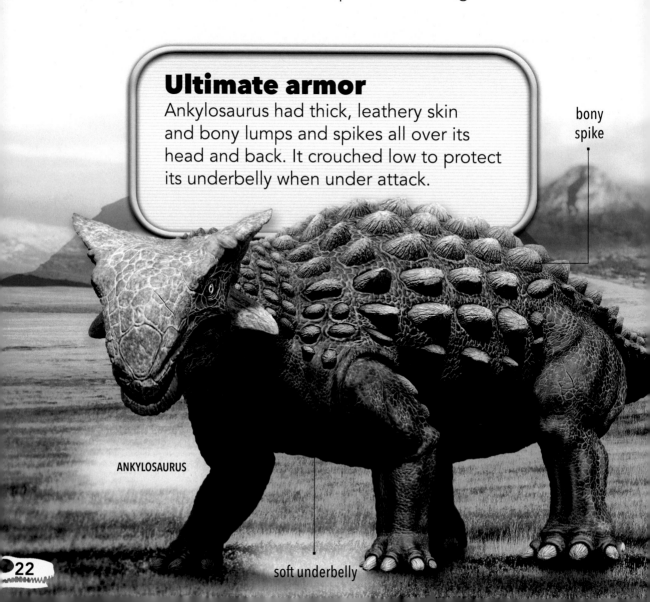

Ultimate armor

Ankylosaurus had thick, leathery skin
and bony lumps and spikes all over its
head and back. It crouched low to protect
its underbelly when under attack.

bony
spike

ANKYLOSAURUS

soft underbelly

Deadly defenses

Stegosaurus had a thick tail that bristled with four large spikes. To defend itself, it turned its back on attackers and swung its tail back and forth to give a lethal blow.

Ankylosaurus's tail ended in a heavy, bony club that was up to 4 feet (1.2m) wide. The dinosaur swung its tail at an attacker. One blow was powerful enough to shatter bone, or even kill.

Diplodocus had a long tail that was as thin and flexible as a whip. If attacked, it lashed its tail to and fro. Its weight could land a blow hard enough to knock an attacker off its feet.

heavy, clubbed tail

RUN FOR YOUR LIFE!

The sound of pounding feet drums across an open plain as a herd of long-legged, birdlike dinosaurs runs for its life. Smaller dinosaurs, such as Caudipteryx, didn't have horns or clubbed tails to defend against meat-eaters, but they could outrun almost any hungry hunter.

Feathered dinosaurs

Caudipteryx had feathers on its tail and arms. It could not fly, but the feathers may have helped it to steer when running quickly to escape predators.

Speed stars

Tiny Compsognathus used its speed to catch lizards or frogs. If hunted by a larger dinosaur, it hid in the undergrowth.

Oviraptor was fast enough to catch lizards or small mammals. It used speed and agility to escape from its enemies, too.

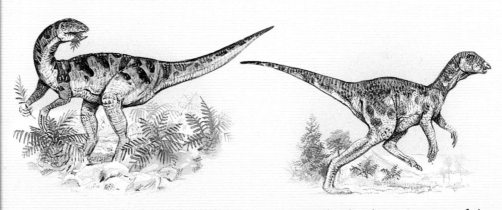

Like all other small plant-eaters, Lesothosaurus relied on the rest of its herd to spot danger, and on its speed to get away.

Hypsilophodon was one of the fastest small plant-eaters. As it fled, it dodged from side to side to escape claws and jaws.

THEN THEY WERE GONE

After ruling the world for 160 million years, the dinosaurs died out. Why? It's most likely that they became extinct after a meteorite smashed into Earth, exploding with the power of a thousand volcanoes. The explosion killed everything for thousands of miles. Dust from the explosion blacked out the Sun's light and heat. Earth became cold, and many creatures—including the dinosaurs—perished.

Explosion

1. A huge meteorite 6 miles (9.6km) wide and traveling at 60,000 miles per hour (96,560kph), hit Earth in Central America.

2. It formed a crater almost 120 miles (193km) wide and threw a massive cloud of dust into the sky.

3. The dust blocked out the sunlight for many years. The air became cold. Many plants and animals died.

TYRANNOSAURUS REX

Dinosaur survivors

Many scientists think dinosaurs were the ancestors of today's birds.

Avimimus–a fast, feathered dinosaur

Roadrunner–a relative of Avimimus?

BIG BURIED BONES

We know about the dinosaurs that lived millions of years ago because of clues they left behind, such as fossils of their bones, teeth, and claws. When fossils of dinosaur bones are discovered, scientists called paleontologists clear away the rock that surrounds them. The scientists also measure and photograph the fossils.

How fossils are made

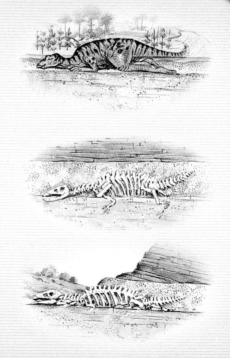

1. Millions of years ago, a dinosaur died. It was buried under soft sand or mud.

2. The skin and flesh rotted away, but the hard bones slowly became fossils, and the sand and mud surrounding them turn into rock.

3. The rock containing the fossils is worn away by wind and rain, and the fossils appeared at the surface.

Fossils on view

Some fossils are are removed and displayed in museums. Others are left in the ground for people to see where the dinosaur once roamed.

BONE PUZZLE

When the fossilized bones of a dinosaur arrive at a museum, scientists use special tools to clean the debris from them. Then the scientists piece together the bones to try to build a complete skeleton.

All kinds of fossils

Scientists often find fossils of footprints. How big and how far apart the footprints are tell us how large and how fast the dinosaur was. We also have fossils of dinosaur eggs, fossils that show scaly skin, and even fossils of dinosaur dung!

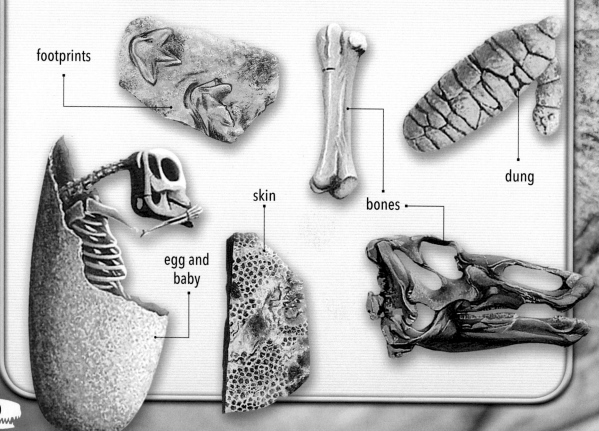

footprints

dung

skin

bones

egg and baby

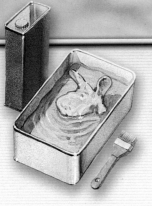

In the museum

1. If the fossil is in a rock called limestone, it may be given a bath in weak vinegar to help wash away some of the rock.

2. Dentist's drills and toothpicks are used to clean the last traces of rock from each bone. A dinosaur has over 300 bones, so it can take months to do this delicate job.

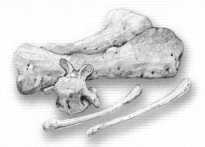

3. Fossils are old and can crumble easily. Scientists paint them with chemicals to strengthen them and protect them from dust or dirt.

4. The bones are compared with others, so scientists can decide whether they are from a new kind of dinosaur or a known one.

5. Steel rods or wires hold the heavy bones in position. Plastic bones are made if some of the bones are missing. Once the skeleton has been completed, scientists figure our how muscles held the bones together, how skin covered the muscles, and what the dinosaur looked like when it was alive.

Camarasaurus skeleton

GLOSSARY

armor A thick layer of bone under the skin of some dinosaurs. This prevented hunters from biting through the skin.

climate The usual, year-round weather of a place. In jungles, the climate is hot and wet, but in deserts the climate is dry.

colony A group of animals that comes together to lay eggs and raise young. A colony is harder for a hunter to attack than a single animal.

Cretaceous The third and last great age of dinosaurs, which lasted from 145 to 66 million years ago. By the end of it, all dinosaurs had died out.

dinosaurs Large, land-living reptiles of the Triassic, Jurassic, or Cretaceous periods. The name is from the Ancient Greek for "terrible lizard."

duckbills A group of plant-eating dinosaurs that had wide snouts like a duck's bill.

extinction The death of every last one of a group of plants or animals. The dinosaurs became extinct 66 million years ago.

fossil The remains of an ancient plant or animal. All we know about dinosaurs comes from their fossils.

herd A large group of animals. Many dinosaurs lived in herds for protection—a herd has many eyes and ears to detect an attacker.

Jurassic The second great age of dinosaurs, from 201 to 145 million years ago.

meat-eater An animal that eats other animals, by killing them or by feeding on already dead bodies.

meteorite A chunk of rock that hurtles through space and crashes to Earth. Most are so small that we hardly notice them. The few big ones cause huge explosions.

paleontologist A scientist who studies ancient plants and animals—mainly from fossils that are millions of years old.

plant-eater An animal that feeds on plants, not on other animals. Most dinosaurs were plant-eaters. So are most animals today.

predator An animal that hunts other animals.

prey An animal that is being hunted by another animal.

reptile A coldblooded, scaly animal that lays its eggs on land. Dinosaurs were reptiles. So are lizards, snakes, crocodiles, and turtles.

sauropods The name for all large, long-necked, plant-eating dinosaurs, such as Diplodocus.

skeleton The framework of bones that holds up the body of any animal.

Triassic The first of the three great ages of dinosaurs, from 252 to 201 million years ago.

INDEX